CPSIA information can be obtained at www.ICGtesting.com
Printed in the USA
LVIW01n2121280416
485840LV00008B/26

The Great Adventures of Nina Puppalina and Lizzy Lou: Nina Finds Her Home

Are you ready for our adventure?

For Elizabeth Louise –D.W.S.

For Skylar –S.A.

Author acknowledgements...

I want to thank my husband Wes, daughter Elizabeth Louise, and Nina Puppalina who inspire and encourage me in all my efforts! To our families and friends for their support. Thanks to my amazing publishing consultant, Damaris Curran Herlihy, and intensely talented illustrator, Sarah Ashmun, for believing in my vision and working tirelessly along side me to create this series. A special thanks to Clark Martin, Paige Martin, Vanessa Bourgeois, Kari Miller, Amy Steele, Anne Curran, Sally Fuller, Sheila Moreau, Cristine Ragland, Beth Zerilli, Alyssa Englis, Erin Obernesser, Allison Mueller, Sally Trudgeon, Angie Gunter, the Heymann-Herz family, and the Reed-Gaytan family.

A message from the illustrator ...

My love for art began at a young age. I have been drawing on paper, canvas, and even walls since I was three years old! Experimenting with different drawing tools like colored pencils, markers, and paints all at once is my favorite way to create illustrations. For *The Great Adventures of Nina Puppalina and Lizzy Lou*, I have enjoyed sharing my vision of a doggy-dream world by interpreting how a puppy sees his or her environment. Our furry friends see the colors blue, green, and purple more vividly than we do. They also see more of the world around them in a single glance! This is called a panoramic view and is very different from how we see our surroundings. Since their eyes are on the sides of their heads, dogs can also see more detail in their side vision and less detail directly in front of them. From these stories, I hope you will learn some of the differences between a dog's vision and ours. The world can be a magical place when viewed through a different lens.

A message from the author ...

I have always enjoyed creative writing! When our daughter Elizabeth was a toddler, I became obsessed with finding great stories with beautiful illustrations to read at night. In our family, storytelling is encouraged at bedtime, too, so we often make up our own stories. When we adopted Nina, our daughter was four and a half years old. Elizabeth didn't understand how to behave around our new, furry friend and, despite my constant reminders, the message was not registering. I decided to write *The Great Adventures of Nina Puppalina and Lizzy Lou* from the puppy's perspective, to help Elizabeth understand how her puppy felt. Thankfully it worked and my nagging reminders ceased! Upon completing my first manuscript, I did further research on how dogs see, smell, and feel the world around them. This research required me to rewrite my original story many times until it felt just right. It is my hope that we encourage other families to adopt pets.

There are a multitude of wonderful pet-rescue organizations and adoption fairs to help you find just the right furry friend for your family. To learn more about pet adoption, please visit Nina's website (www.ninapuppalina.com/resources).

My delicious dinner makes
me sleepy. As I fall asleep,
I think to myself, I love my
new family—especially Lizzy
Lou! I am home indeed! I lick
her sugary, delectable cheek
to say goodnight. She says,
"Good night, Nina Puppalina.
You are my new best friend.
I'm so glad we found you. I
will always love you!" I tell her
I will always love her, too!

I dream that we do catch the
butterfly. We ride on its wings
through the starry night. We
watch the breathtaking earth
below. Sweet dreams, my
Lizzy Lou … and good night.

My new mom tells Lizzy Lou it is time to feed me.
She scoops up a bowl full of puppy chow. I am the
luckiest dog in the world!

I smell something yummy. It reminds me that I'm hungry! I follow the scent.

A marvelous, swallowtail butterfly flutters in the breeze. It has many shades of blue and black with bright spots. Lizzy Lou and I leap into the air as we chase its wings. We try very hard but neither of us catch it.

Lizzy Lou and I play fetch. We chase each other through the wide, open yard. She laughs as she chases me. I bark and wag my tail so she knows I am having fun, too!

It's a brilliant, warm, sunny day. I chase my wagging tail in circles! I jump into Lizzy Lou's arms. I am so pleased to be here.

My new dad takes me out of the crate.
Cookie crumbs cover my whiskers. He tells
Lizzy Lou I am not allowed to eat anything
but special dog food. Lizzy Lou gives me a
wink that makes my heart sing! ♪♫♪ ♫♪

We stop in front of a house with a lovely front porch. Lizzy Lou tells me her neighborhood friends, Herbie and Santiago, are waiting on the porch to meet me. This must be my new home! I hope I can stay here forever.

As we drive along, Lizzy Lou is eating cookies with sprinkles on top. She shares a cookie with me. It is tasty! I can smell the honeysuckle blooming outside. I see green trees blowing in the breeze. It's magnificent to my eyes.

Lizzy Lou puts me in a new crate for the journey to our home. I lay down on a warm, soft blanket that smells lovely just like Lizzy Lou. The scent makes me so happy.

She hugs me very tight, giving me all of her love. She giggles and shouts, "Nina Puppalina, we will be best friends!"

The little girl's eyes sparkle. She whispers in my ear. "My name is Lizzy Lou! And your name is Nina Puppalina!" Oh, my new name is glorious!

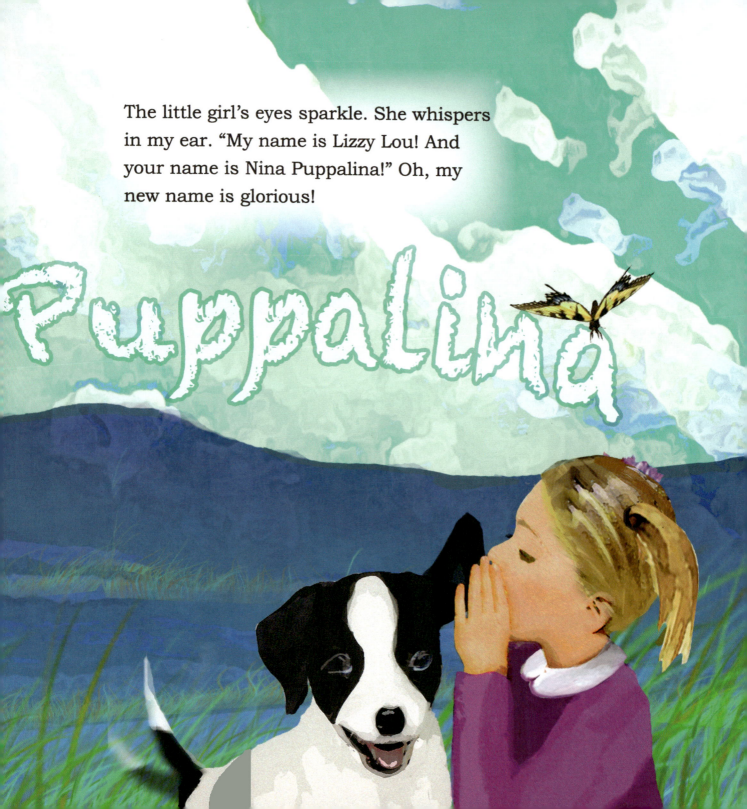

Puppalina

I feel warm and very content with the little girl. Is this my new family? Could it be? It must be!

Nina

She picks me up and almost drops me. That scares me! She sits on the floor and I jump into her lap. She smells like something sweet! What is that delicious smell? I could sniff her all day long.

Then I see the happiest sight I've ever seen. She is a cheerful, little girl with a big, purple flower in her hair. She is delighted to see me! We are both jumping up and down with joy! Will she want to play with me?

They have bright, warm smiles. They kneel down to look into my eyes. Their hands smell and taste delicious. Do they like me as much as I like them?

Suddenly I see a face smiling right at me! I bark, "Over here!" He is a dad with a blue baseball hat. He hears my bark and comes to me. Holding his hand is a mom looking at me with adoring eyes.

I keep my eyes open to the world. I want to see all the new faces around me. Who will like me? Who will want to play with me? I know my new family is here somewhere.

Oh me, oh my! My brothers and sisters are being taken away! They're going to new families, but a new family hasn't found me yet. It's taking too long.

I see many new people, too.
Their faces are very friendly
and kind. When they pet my
fur, their touch feels good. I
especially like it when they
scratch me under my chin.

I smell wet fur in the air.
I see many dogs. They are
young and old, big and little.

Where are we? The nice people from our farm tell us we're here in the city to find new families. What does that mean? I love my family on the farm! Will I love my new family, too?

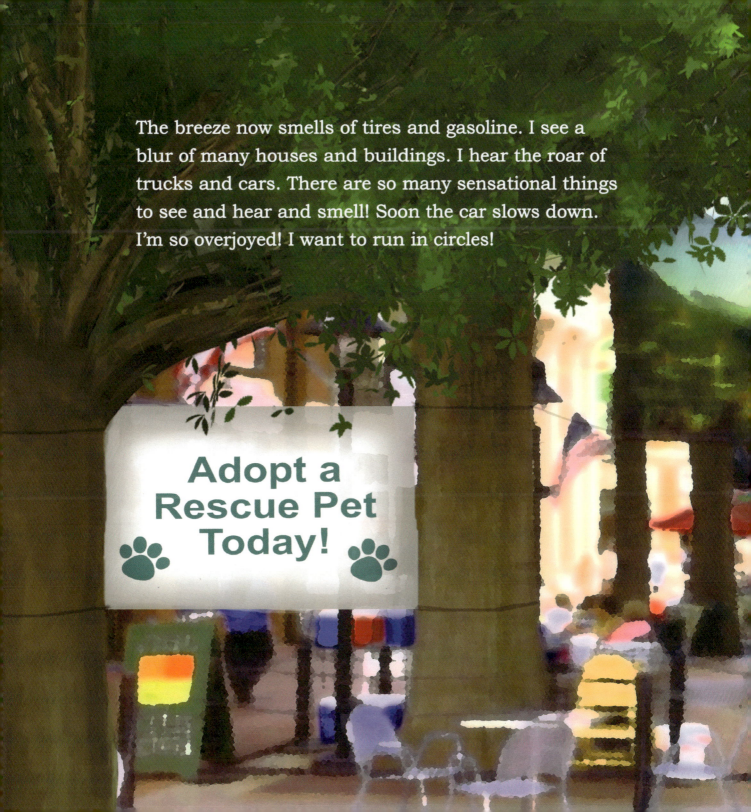

The breeze now smells of tires and gasoline. I see a blur of many houses and buildings. I hear the roar of trucks and cars. There are so many sensational things to see and hear and smell! Soon the car slows down. I'm so overjoyed! I want to run in circles!

Adopt a Rescue Pet Today!

I look out the window. There are wide, open fields as far as my eyes can see. Green grass and purple flowers blow in the breeze as we whiz by. I'm nervous but also very excited!

I smell fresh-cut grass in the morning air. The warm breeze from the open window tickles my nose. I wag my happy tail and wrestle with my brothers and sisters.

It's a beautiful day outside. I'm playing with my brothers and sisters on the farm. I hear the birds singing in the trees. The nice man on the farm ushers us into crates for a car ride. I love car rides! I wonder where we are going. Why are we leaving our farm?